The Kittiwakes' Warning

MIKE PEARCE

Copyright 2018 by Mike Pearce

All rights reserved. No part of this book may be reproduced, distributed or transmitted in any form or by any means, including photocopying, recording, or other electronic or mechanical methods, without the prior written permission of the author, except in the case of brief quotations embodied in reviews and certain other non-commercial uses permitted by copyright law. You must not circulate this book in any format.

This book may not be resold or given away to other people. Please respect the work of the author and purchase a copy for you own use.

This is a fictional work and all characters are drawn from the author's imagination. Any resemblance or similarities to persons living or dead are entirely coincidental

DEDICATION

This book is dedicate to all those that are concerned about the loss of many of our buildings and monuments from the past by weathering. Also to those who show concern for the Kittiwakes who in some cities are not accepted as inhabitants.

.

CONTENTS

ACKNOWLEDGMENTS

The author would like to thank Christine Pearce
for reading and checking through the manuscript.

PREFACE

Many people will have visited towns and resorts where buildings such as cathedrals and town halls and other structures are made out of white or brown sandstone. This is mainly due to the availability in the area. The buildings all look magnificent but over time weathering has made them pitted, scarified and blackened with many of the fine features lost.

Kittiwakes often nest on such structures. They can see what is happening, but their cry remains unheard as the weathering continues today. This story is about a pair of kittiwakes who witness the demise of their nesting places which they had had for so many years.

1 USES OF SANDSTONE

In the past sacred stones were erected often with markings on them but these diminished in size and broke into several pieces. Sandstone is one of the most common sedimentary rocks. It was used for a lot of religious buildings especially in the 12th century when abbeys expanded to have cloisters and kitchens together with warming rooms to protect them from the harsh winters. A lot of temples were also made of white sandstone while a hundred years later brown sandstone became more common.

Two kittiwakes arrived from the northern Atlantic. They were only medium sized gulls and had grey upper feathers. Their legs were shorter than the herring gulls, their hind toes only a bump. Their wing tips are all black without a white patch. They had spent the winter around the northern Atlantic feeding on sand eels. Travelling thousands of miles daily, they had returned to nest. At this time chapels, churches and town buildings were still being built of sandstone, even the monks have sandstone blocks for seats. The sandstone window frames often contained stained glass depicting Celtic or Saxon scenes of valour, defeating enemies or even dragons and the walls were whitewashed and covered in paintings.

The problem with some sandstones they are highly absorbant, often get wet, then dry. Water may not be absorbed entirely though as the pores are not aligned throughout the stone. Trapped water however can freeze or expand by thermal expansion if in the sun. Pollution can also form nd outside skin with the sandstone disintegrating unnoticed underneath. Some stones may also contain crystals of quartz or calcite in its structure it may even be coloured e.g. reds from iron which can leach out. The pounding of salt filled rain near the coast does not help. The salt can crystallise when the sandstone dries out. Also stability is affected if there is a lot of clay between the grains of sand. One can see the effect of weathering of sandstone in the Grand Canyon or in Petra in Southern Jordan.

Each year the kittiwakes had noticed how the

structures they flew past had, in some places, crumbled or been destroyed by weathering. On gravestones the rain had seeped through the top and vertical layers split and broke off. Algae and pollution also had not helped. They also saw how easy it was for the sandstone to be gouged out through internal or foreign conflicts, cannon or rifle fire, even gunpowder explosions. Man had not helped in some cases by emitting pollutants especially in the 19th century into the air forming weak acid rain which could eat through the stone. Sometimes an empty outer skin layer remains over the sandstone, but this can trap water underneath which can be frozen and expand in winter cracking the stone.

2 THE NEED FOR NESTING SITES

The birds were concerned over some of the forms of wear. Often stones were left oddly shaped having single or multiple pits in them of varying depths. Many were honeycombed with little caverns and where thin like thin stone lace. Carvings on the sides of buildings and statues of famous people or saints had lost the features of their faces. The saddest thing was sandstone gravestones no longer held the names of the people who were commemorated there which was their purpose. Even forfamous people, the names were obliterated forever. Other gravestone seemed to withstand the pace of time such as those made out of granite or hard limestones.

As the years went by more and more kittiwakes returned to nest. They liked to build their nests on ledges e.g. on window sills or other projecting features on buildings. This reminded them of the narrow cliff edges where they used to nest in the past. They were now a protected species unlike the herring gulls who only had a general licence.

The pair always built their nest out of seaweed and mud. Their nest was on the window sill of a very large and expensive hotel in town facing away from the sea. This particular ledge had been theirs for many years and other birds were chased off. It wasn't very wide and there had even been plastic spikes put along the outer edge, but these were ignored and covered by nesting materials. Other kittiwakes, some of them relatives, were on the other window sills on this back side of the building. There hundreds of others nesting on the ledges of the buildings in extensive rows next to one another but with spacings.

The kittiwake pair produced two buff coloured grey/reddish brown speckled eggs which hatched in about a month. From then on, they took turns in fetching food for the young. They caught sand eels dipping their heads in the water and scooping up fish with their special tongues.

Some of their neighbours never had partners but they behaved just as though they had young and went away to forage and came back to their window sill. The paired gulls, when one returned, would be greeted by a cry which, with all the other cries, resembled very young children being let out at playtime.

3 A WARNING CRY

This cry of KITE-WA-WAKE from which they got their name echoed around the town accompanied by a lot of head nodding and pecking rituals normally seem in gulls. The problems found by all kittiwakes was that the sills of the hotel were made of sandstone as were most of the other buildings at this seaside resort. Sandstone in one way was good as it was a warmer stone than other stone so helped to raise the nest temperature. The chicks though were satisfied with such a narrow window sill platform to wander about on and were very adept at not falling off the ledges.

Some buildings had put up netting to prevent them nesting. Others had UV light emmitters which the birds did not like. The number of available nesting places was diminishing each year as much of the sandstone was crumbling away and the ledges gone. Some birds had found refuge on the supports of a walkway running from the beach to the town but here it it was really cramped, the nests sitting very close to each other and the ledges were even slimmer. These ledges were made of concrete not sandstone. The town was expanding, new buildings were being constructed all the time, new office blocks as well as shops in town were being constructed. Sandstone was still being used because of it nice appearance.

It was the time of Folk week. The town was bustling with people of all ages. There was entertainment and classes. Many people were camped out on the fields of schools. It was a disturbing time for the kittiwakes. Music was everywhere and each public house and hotel seemed to have some sort of entertainment going on well into the night. Herring gulls enjoyed this time as there were always scraps of food around to take away. But as for the kittiwakes they preferred to get their food from the sea.

It was Saturday night, time for the folk procession where performers would march down the high street dancing and playing instruments. Leading the procession was a large green dragons head worn by one of the folk week organisers. There were also little black wooden dragon heads held up with a pole with moveable mouths which would pretend to bite onlookers. The kittiwakes stopped their foraging whilst the procession proceeded. and remained quiet while dancers hit metal rods or wooden sticks. Some dancers waved their handkerchiefs whilst others waved flowered covered hoops. A small group would stop their walking and throw down wooden boards in front of them and start tap dancing on these to music. Many a squeeze box, accordion, penny whistles and violin sounded out as the people moved down the street towards the seafront.

This was bearable for the kittiwakes, better than the nights they had the firework displays. Most of the fireworks produced loud bangs shaking the buildings and hotels where they were perched. The kittiwakes were not sure of the bells which many dancers had attached to the bottoms of their white trousers. The noise reminded them of the bells they had heard on the beach from the donkeys in previous years or the cart horses that used to travel down the cobbled streets. They also were wary of some performers who had feathers in their hats, blackened faces and wore black clothes. At least the procession was now in the day not at night as it previously was when people carried torches and lanterns in their hands. One year they had huge mannequins made of paper mache which rose many feet in height. Some nearly reached the level of their nesting sites frightening the birds which squarked loudly. Thankfully the folk festival only lasted a week and by the end of this week things once again became quiet and normal.

The kittiwake pair's sandstone ledge had completely worn away. They decided to move from what had been their secure nesting site on the hotel window sill into town. Their young would be able to still nest here on the ledges of the new buildings as would all the generations yet to come. The cry of these birds in town still echoes out the warning about building out of sandstone which came too late for many of those buildings in the past. They had to be pulled down or incurred the cost of brick replacements.

So, listen to the constant cry of the birds you

builders, be aware that sandstone structures will not last for ever and could incur a lot of expense in the future. The prospect of climate change with increased temperatures and wetter weather also will be a problem for sandstone structures for years to come.

To see other publications below by the author visit
snappysnappybooks.com

<u>The really, really, really useful series</u>

How to be a Successful Business Weed
How to Deal with Life's Snakes and Ladders
Know Your Students and Build Your Image
Pens for Pops
How to be a Successful Charity Shop
Make up-revealed
Ronnie's Sermon snippets
Wastefulness-Bone and Urine
Fertility Stones and Chocolate Eggs
Clingers, creepers and scramblers
I Herring Gull
Viking Bay-Natural History
Go Fat Go
Hidden from the heart but not forgotten
Pulvi Royal

<u>Other books by Mike Pearce:</u>

Pattern for Purpose- God's and Man's designs
Red Fred Cell and Friends
Human Termites eat London
Pigeons Splat London
Glass Anemones Tentacle-ize London
Tuppeny Hangover
I am Termite
The littlest Oyster
Bits and Bobs
The Shell Man
Cats at Christmas
Tails, Tales
Trust-Nothing but a Must
In a Dark, Dark Corner was the Holy Ghost
The Shell Lady
Captain Grottbuster versus the Grey World
London's Nemesis (Trilogy of 3, 4 and 5 above
Saved by Angels (Trilogy of 6, 8 and 14 above)
The World of Wax
Photosynthetic Women
Queen Rat on Deadman's Island
The Watcher on the Fal
The Rock Pool
The Little Shepherd Boy's Gift
The Living Fossils
Old Mother Nature Laughed and Laughed
Betty's Barcodes

Time Runs Dry (play)
Valentines Cards
The Scrofula Infirmary
The Cornish Urchin
My Therizinosaurus
Spider in the Tomb
The White Cockerel
The Red Church Doll
Butterfly Angels (compilation of previous books)
The Girl Under the Paeony Tree
Baby Feet
The Sparrows' Last Soul
Ball Rooms
Absorbed by a Woman
St Mildred-Patron Saint of Thanet
The Slothful Wife
The Tuppeny Bear
The Boy who found Christmas
Nothing but leaves
The Giant's Toothpick
The Night Mare
The Old Pot and the Golden Shoes
Sitting next to Angels
Exodus to a leaf
The forlorn fruit fly
The Pawnbroker's Souls
The Nursery Rhyme Cat
A Call Under the Sea
Dead Donkey Lane
A Googolplex of Mice
The Eggstraordinary Easter Egg
The China Blackbird
A slice of Slang with a touch of Cockney and a
drop of Dorset

The Rusty Gate
Beware of Cucumbers, apples and pigs
The Lady loves Red
The woman who smelled books
Till my lips were salt as brine
The Giant and the Giraffe Boy
The man who always sprinted
Boy,could she smell!
Coloured bricks
The Lady who loved Hairspray
I'm just going to the bathroom
Screaming Alley
Shepherd's Purse
Two sleepy boys
Mr Hamstrings Dinner

ABOUT THE AUTHOR

Dr Mike Pearce is a scientist interested in behaviour. He also was a lecturer in human biology and health at a college in Canterbury, Kent